→→52←←
WAYS TO
GET
YOUR LIFE
& HOUSE
IN ORDER

Kate Redd

OLIVER
NELSON

THOMAS NELSON PUBLISHERS
Nashville

Published in Nashville, Tennessee, by Oliver-Nelson Books, a division of Thomas Nelson, Inc., Publishers, and distributed in Canada by Lawson Falle, Ltd., Cambridge, Ontario.

Library of Congress Cataloging-in-Publication Data

Redd, Kate.
    52 ways to get your life and house in order / Kate Redd.
      p. cm.
    ISBN 0-8407-9661-7 (pbk.)
    1. Finance, Personal. 2. Time management. 3. Records
—Management. 4. Life skills. I. Title. II. Title: Fifty-two
ways to get your life and house in order.
HG179.R34 1993
332.024—dc20   92-32836
                                                 CIP

Printed in the United States of America.

1 2 3 4 5 6 — 98 97 96 95 94 93

Dedicated to

My mother,
Catherine,

who taught me that order and spontaneity
are not opposites, but that one makes
possible the other, and that both
are to be desired and pursued

Contents

Introduction: It Doesn't Need to Stay This Way!

Are you feeling overwhelmed by too many obligations, too many loose ends, too many "things" to care for, too many bills?

Do you feel as if you have an "overstuffed life," with too much of just about everything, including too many things on your schedule and too many draws against your income?

This book is for you!

The good news for you today is that you *do* have control—probably more than you realize—over these three key areas of your life:

- your schedule,
- your money, and
- your possessions.

You *can* decide how you want to spend your time—at least the majority of it! Even if you work eight hours a day, you have the freedom to decide how you will spend your breaks and the hours each day when you aren't at work. You *can* decide how you want to spend your money. You *can* decide how much stuff you want to own, dust, collect, or store—and how much access you want to it.

To bring a sense of order to your life, you must first make these four decisions:

Choose to Take Control over your time, money, and possessions, rather than let these things control you. The fact is, if you don't take control, you will be controlled.

Choose to Strike a New Balance between input and output, income and expense, incoming and outgoing. We're all involved in a balancing act. We have twenty-four hours a day given to us; we choose how to divide that time into smaller segments and to spend it on various activities. We each have an income; we choose what and how much to purchase with it. We create a "space" for ourselves and decide how to fill it. The more we try to put into a space, get from an income, or do in a day, the more difficult it is to keep a sense of order and balance.

Choose to Put Like Things Together

Keeping like things together is perhaps the greatest thing you can do to achieve a sense of order in your life. As you begin to tackle the challenge of adding more order to your house and life, keep the word *clusters* in mind. Group things together. Store like things together. Put similar tasks together. Cluster errands and chores.

Choose Joy!

If you don't experience a sense of joy and fulfillment from a task, activity, relationship, purchase, process, or possession, let go of it. The purpose for bringing order to your life is not so that you can take on more, acquire more, or do more, but so that you can experience more joy.

Finally, it's important to recognize that every person has a different level of need for order. You may be able to handle a fuller schedule, more details, and more clutter than others. If you are sharing space, schedules, and money with someone, you'll need to find a compromise point. Recognize at the outset that there's no ideal "limit" to the number of pieces, time segments, or units that a person can accommodate successfully. Some people need very few things to feel an inner sense of balance and joy; others need more. Accommodate these differences as best you can. Don't be obsessive in your need for order. At the same time, do gain the sense of order that *you* need to feel control, balance, access, and joy.

Always remember, the number one reason for bringing order to something is so that you can use it and enjoy it to the fullest.

THE BIGGIES

Nine suggestions for gaining
order in the "big picture" of your life

1 ✔ Make a Budget

The best way to gain control over your money and possessions is to make a budget.

Most people know the basics of budget-making, but a surprising number of people have never been taught how to make a budget that reflects a personal financial plan. Let's review the basics.

Decide the Time Frame for Your Budget Most people deal with money on a monthly basis. Others find that a quarterly budget suits them best. For others, an annual or semi-annual overview gives order. If you are planning a two-week vacation, you may want to make a budget to cover only that time period.

If you are self-employed, or have income that fluctuates from month to month, you may find that it helps to make both monthly and quarterly budgets.

List All Your Sources of Income Make two categories: the "sure" sources, and the "possible" sources. If there's at least a twenty-percent chance that the amount won't be there in a given time frame, put it in the "possible" category. In constructing your budget, consider that you will only receive eighty percent of your income in the "possible" category. If you find at the end of the month that you've got more income than anticipated, set aside a portion of it for additional taxes and then use the remainder for investments.

If you are self-employed, you need to make certain that a portion of every income check is set aside for quarterly tax payments.

List Your Expenses   Begin with your fixed expenses. These are amounts that remain the same from month to month. Then, estimate those items that tend to fluctuate, such as utilities, food, gasoline, phone, clothing, and so forth. Don't overlook these key areas among your expenses:

- *Contributions.* Many people pledge to give a set amount to their church or other not-for-profit organization on a regular basis. Include that figure among your fixed expenses.

- *Savings.* Include savings in the fixed category, even if it's a small amount. Pay yourself this amount off the top and put it into a separate, interest-bearing account.

- *Annualized or Periodic Payments.* This is an area that many people fail to budget properly. As a result, they find themselves in a cash-flow crunch.

In order to get a handle on this area of your finances, make a list of all of your anticipated annual or semiannual expenses, such as insurance premiums, car maintenance, etc.

If you are saving for a major purchase, such as an appliance, piece of furniture, or vehicle, add that item to your list. If you are saving for a child's college education, also add the amount you want to save to this list.

Add all of these amounts together, as best you can estimate them, and then divide by twelve. This gives you the amount each month that you need to set aside. Put this money into an interest-bearing checking or savings account. Then, when these expenses roll around, pay them from this separate account.

Credit Cards   Avoid their use. Your life will become a lot simpler, and probably less expensive. If you use credit cards, aim to pay them off.

2 ✔ Make a Will

One of the most difficult things for many people to do, and yet one of the most important for getting your life in order, is to make a will. Don't think of your will as something morbid or sad. Think of it strictly in financial-planning, possession-planning, and people-caring terms.

By planning for your departure from this world, you'll be helping those you love in a tremendous way, releasing them from the burden of making major decisions in their sorrow, saving them unnecessary expense, and making sure that each person you want to remember materially is properly regarded. Furthermore, by making decisions about your death when you are healthy, you are saving yourself the added emotional burden that can arise in having to face such decisions while battling a serious illness or injury.

Your Legal Will Work with an attorney in constructing your will. Although many self-help forms are available and can give you a good start in making your plans, you should still consult an attorney. An attorney will be able to ask you questions about issues you may not have considered, and also be able to suggest alternatives and innovative methods of planning your estate.

A Living Will Decide whether you want to have a living will. This document states that if the situation should arise in which there is no reasonable expectation of your recovery from physical or mental disability, you request that you be allowed to die and not be kept alive by artificial means or heroic measures. Most physicians and clergymen have forms, as do attorneys.

Disposition of Your Body Do you want to donate your body organs for transplant purposes to help others? Do you want to give your body to help medical schools in their research and in training of future physicians? Do you wish to be buried, or cremated?

Funeral Arrangements It will take you less than an hour to plan your funeral, and save your loved ones a great deal of anguish. List your favorite Scriptures or readings, your choice of flowers and music. State whom you would like to conduct the service or have part in it (including pallbearers, soloists, organist). Describe the nature of the service (memorial service, graveside service, closed-casket).

General Information   In a file along with
your will, living will, and funeral arrangements,
you may want to provide this information for your
survivors:

- Obituary information. Jot down key dates,
  places, and events of your life, as well as
  the names of all close relatives.

- Location of key documents, bank accounts,
  insurance policies, name of attorney.

- A list of persons to notify about your death.

- A list of any bequests you'd like to see
  made beyond the scope of your will. You
  may have small personal items of sentimen-
  tal value that you'd like to go to specific
  persons. Bear in mind that, unless these
  items are stated in your formal will, the bequests you desire are not legally binding.

You may want to discuss this information with
others in your family. Or, you may simply want to
let key members of your family know that you
have made such plans. Let them know where
they can find the file of your final wishes after
your death.

Once you have a will and a set of final wishes in
place, you'll probably experience a great sense of
relief and a feeling that something important has
been put in order.

3 ✔ Keep Important Documents in a Safe Place

Every person needs a safe place to keep important documents. You may want to have a locked, fire-proof safe installed in your basement or an interior closet. Have your key documents grouped together in this safe for quick access.

A safety deposit box in a local bank or savings organization is perhaps the best place to keep your important documents, or at least a copy of them. You may also want to have a copy of key documents on file in the home of a close relative.

Ask yourself, "If I had only ten minutes to evacuate my home, could I put my hands on key documents within the first sixty seconds?" Ask:

- What do I need to have, should my house be completely destroyed?

- What do I need to be able to put my hands on, should I not have access to my house?

Hotel Safety Deposit Boxes   When traveling, take advantage of the safety deposit boxes provided by hotels for your key belongings (such as passport, traveler's checks, and jewelry).

4 ✔ Reappraise Your Insurance Coverage

Periodically reappraise your insurance coverage. The need for various types of insurance fluctuates greatly during a lifetime. Types of insurance policies being offered tend to vary greatly from decade to decade.

Don't assume that your insurance agent automatically will want to talk you into increasing your coverage if you make an appointment to discuss your policies. If that's your first assumption, consider finding a new agent! You may want to seek out a general financial planner who includes insurance as only one aspect of a broader financial planning service.

Focus on the details of your current situation and your current policies. Think in terms of your needs during the next three-to-five years, then reevaluate. Ask:

Do I Need This Insurance? Weigh the risks of not having a particular type of insurance. For example, if you have no dependents and no large debts or mortgages for which you are responsible, you should seriously weigh your need for life insurance. If you are self-employed, consider your need for long-term disability insurance.

Which Type of Financial Vehicle Is Best?
Insurance is not the only vehicle that provides income to beneficiaries, or a source of money against which to borrow in emergencies. Weigh the pros and cons of whole-life policies versus term insurance. Have someone list the advantages and disadvantages for you in clear, easily understood terms. Don't think in terms of national averages or typical cases; evaluate the coverage and benefits in terms of your own life and needs. Nobody knows your total financial picture better than you do. Ask a financial planner about alternatives to insurance in providing for retirement income. Ask about other ways of planning your estate to benefit your survivors.

Are My Deductibles Too Low?
If you are paying premiums for the lowest possible deductible on the highest amount of coverage, the chances are that you will pay out a great deal more than you will ever recover in claims. In fact, if you make too many low-deductible claims, you may find your policy being cancelled or your rates increased. Use insurance not as a means of covering small accidents or losses, but of covering major illnesses, injuries, or losses. Your savings account should be built up enough to cover small losses.

Is My Coverage Adequate? If you have young children, and both you and your spouse are working to make ends meet, you probably will need more life insurance than if you and your spouse are both retired or your children are through their formal schooling and are financially independent. If you are retirement age, weigh the possibilities of supplemental health insurance policies that extend coverage beyond what Medicare will pay.

Social Security Request a statement from the Social Security Administration every three-to-five years. Forms are available at your local Social Security office. The statement will tell you how much has been credited to your account. Compare that figure to the totals that have been deducted from your payroll checks, or your self-employment deposits. Keep in mind that human error is always possible in recording information; computers are only as good as those who input the raw data.

Insurance Files Keep all your insurance policies together in your filing system for quick access. Duplicate copies of summary pages for policies and keep them in your safety deposit box or fireproof files. Include as part of your files proof that the current premiums have been paid.

5 ✔ Plan for Your Retirement

Most people dream of their retirement years in terms of how they'd like to spend their time and where they'd like to live or travel. The keys to a successful retirement are having the health to enjoy one's retirement years and the money to pay for what one chooses to do. Both health and finances take planning, not dreaming.

The time to plan for your retirement is now, no matter how young you may be.

Set Specific Retirement Goals   Set a specific annual income. List a particular locale where you'd like to retire. As a part of your plan, state how you'd like to live—the amount of energy and health you want to have, and what activities you specifically want to be able to do.

You need to have a target to aim at! Only with specific goals can you map out a specific plan for reaching them.

Balance Your Current Need for Cash and Your Future Need for Security   You obviously need to live between now and the day you retire. Develop a strategy that balances your current needs and your eventual goals. If you are young, you will probably want to consider the purchase of a home as a long-range investment that can help secure your retirement later.

Develop a Retirement Fund   Be certain it accrues tax-free.

A Strategy for Long-Term Wellness   Retirement means very little unless you have good health to enjoy those years. Health takes planning. Make an appointment with your family physician solely to discuss preventive health care strategies.

Your personal family physician can help you map out a strategy of exercise, diet, and personal habits that has the best possible likelihood of not only extending the length of your life, but the quality of your life.

Planning for your future helps to order your current financial and fiscal fitness regimen. In setting goals and planning strategies for retirement, you will come to grips with your current financial and physical needs, goals, and habits. Thinking in terms of retirement is like drawing the outline to a picture. It gives you a framework for making individual choices about how to color in or define the details of your present life. Without such an outline, it's difficult to make long-range choices or to build life-long habits.

6 ✔ Conduct a Household Inventory

As a precursor to planning for your home insurance needs, you will want to develop a thorough household inventory.

House Plan Keep a copy of your house plans, or make a scale drawing. Not only will this be valuable to you in event of damage to your home, but you will find it helpful should you need to make repairs or wish to remodel.

Photographic Coverage One of the easiest ways to do a household inventory is with a still or video camera. Photograph every area of your house so that all appliances and pieces of furniture are visible. Also photograph the exterior of your home, including any patio or poolside furniture, and any buildings or storage areas that are not attached to your house. Label each photo by room and correlate it to a written description.

You may want to give this job to a budding young camera buff in your family.

A Written Description   Provide a written description of each major item in your home. If possible, provide the cost of the item when purchased, and the year of purchase. If you have inherited or purchased antiques, give as much information about an item as you can. If an item has a serial number, record it.

Jewelry and Personal Items   Photograph and describe all pieces of jewelry or valuable personal clothing.

Collections   If you have a collection, describe it thoroughly, and photograph it.

Don't overlook your family library as a collection. List the titles to all of your books, records, videotapes, cassettes, and compact discs. Use 3″ × 5″ cards, so that you can put your inventories into alphabetical order or specific categories. Estimate the total number of books or other items you own and give an average dollar figure to each item. (The cost of replacing a library or music collection is going to be much more than you have probably anticipated!)

Vehicles   Be sure to include descriptions of your vehicles, including outdoor equipment such as lawn mowers.

Other Property If you own vacation property or rental properties, make a periodic inventory of them. A set of interior photographs prior to the renting of property to others can provide solid evidence should a dispute arise about the refunding of a cleaning or security deposit.

Receipts Keep receipts for major items of furniture or valuable antiques, paintings, and jewelry.

Updates You'll want to update your household inventory at least once every three-to-five years, or as you make additional major purchases. Keep a copy of the photos or videotape, and the accompanying written description, in your safety deposit box.

7 ✔ Put It on the Calendar

Gaining a sense of control over time and getting your schedule in order require one basic tool: a calendar. Buy or make a calendar that meets your needs. You may need a calendar that breaks a day down into fifteen-minute increments; you may need a calendar that allows only a little bit of space for each day. You'll want a calendar that allows you to plan your activities most effectively. For example, you may want a calendar that shows an entire week at a time, or a month, or a quarter, or a year.

Focus on one calendar format for recording your commitments. For example, if your calendar shows a week at a time, you may still want to have annual or quarterly calendars available for reference. Record all your commitments only on the weekly format calendar. Don't attempt to juggle more than one calendar format at a time. Even more important, limit yourself to one personal calendar. Don't have a calendar at home and another at work. Keep one calendar and carry it with you or have ready access to it at home, at work, and as you travel.

Family Calendars You may find it necessary to have a master family calendar in addition
to your personal calendar. If so, develop a habit of
going over that calendar on a regular basis—
weekly or daily—with other members of the family, to make certain that everyone knows when
and where they need to be. Have a periodic Family Calendar Pow-Wow, in which every member of
the family goes over the upcoming week's events,
or looks ahead to an entire month or season. This
can be especially beneficial as you enter a holiday
season, or anticipate the events of summer.

A Commitment to Scheduling Discuss
those events that may be happening in your community, church, or other groups to which you be-
long, and make a decision about whether you
want to participate. If you'd like to keep the event
as an option, you may want to write it down in
parentheses or label it as a *maybe*.

Calendar Control You control the calendar;
the calendar doesn't control you. If you find that
you or your family is feeling over-scheduled or
over-committed, get out the eraser and free up
some time.

8 ✔ Write It Down!

Perhaps the single most beneficial thing you can do to add order to your life is to develop a habit of writing lists. Not only will you be freeing up memory space in your own brain, you'll gain a better handle on how to structure your time, finances, and possessions.

A List Is a Tool The reason for a list is to help you remember to do something, or to help you make a decision. There's nothing that's too big or small for a list, if such a list is *helpful* to you.

Cluster and Prioritize One of the most helpful aspects of list-making is that it allows you to cluster like activities together, and then to prioritize them.

- List all of your calls. At the same time, decide whom you need to call first.

- List all the things you need to do this morning. As you list them, decide what order to do them in.

- List the projects you need to complete. You now have the basic foundation needed for dividing tasks into doable steps, setting periodic deadlines, and juggling more than one project at once.

Side-by-side lists of personal things to do and professional things to do can help you balance your home and work lives. Listing the things you hope to complete in a week can help you pare down and prioritize your work load.

A list can also help you develop a new habit. If there's something you'd like to make a part of your daily routine, list it! You'll be focusing your attention on that task and there's a far greater likelihood that you'll make time for it. A time of morning prayer, kissing your spouse before you leave for work, telling your child you love her, flossing at night—no habit is too small to list if it's truly something you consider important to your life.

Completing a List Don't feel compelled to complete a list before you revise it, make a new one, or add to it. Lists aren't records of accomplishment; they are tools for planning, prioritizing, and scheduling. Don't become so list absorbed that you spend all of your creative energy writing down what you want to do, and then fail to get in gear and do those things. A list is only as good as the results it produces.

9 ✔ Live Free of Guilt and Bitterness

All of the planning, sorting, and organizing you do won't help you live an ordered life if you don't find a way of dealing with guilt and bitterness. Guilt stems from what you feel *you* should have done, or shouldn't have done. Bitterness grows from a feeling that *someone else* should or shouldn't have done something.

The real purpose for having order in life is to develop a sense of control over the controllables, and a resulting feeling of balance, accomplishment, and joy. Nothing robs a person of control, balance, fulfillment, or joy, as much as guilt and bitterness.

Eliminating Guilt and Bitterness The only way to get rid of guilt and bitterness is through forgiveness. Forgiveness begins with recognition that you have said or done something that violates your concept of the type of person you really want to be. Face up to that shortfall. If it's a sin against your Creator, apologize and ask for help in not repeating the offense. If it's a sin against your neighbor, apologize and seek to make amends.

Once you have a sense of forgiveness from God, forgive yourself and get on with your life. Don't live in the past or let the past cast a shadow on your future. If you ask forgiveness of a person who refuses to forgive you or refuses to allow you to make amends, face up to the fact that you have done all you can do. Move forward in your life.

Forgiveness Brings Order to a Relationship It heals. It restores. There's an accompanying sense of freedom, which allows a person to face the future with a positive outlook. New choices can be made that can bring a greater sense of balance, fulfillment, and joy.

SPACE CONTROL

Seven suggestions for bringing
order to your space

10 ✔ Forming Clusters

A major key in ordering your possessions is to put like things together in a separate container or area.

Containers A variety of containers can be used for sorting items of all types. Use your imagination! Clear plastic sweater boxes, clean tool boxes, cash boxes, or artist supply boxes can all be used in innovative ways. Baby food jars are excellent containers for buttons, safety pins and straight pins, paper clips, picture-hanging nails, and other small items. Baskets are excellent for clustering pens and pencils, sewing or hobby supplies, magazines, photographs, stationery, hair ornaments, or business cards. Plastic file boxes, rolling baskets, and various types of bins can be used for storing children's art supplies, toys, and books, clothing, office supplies, and craft projects. Large mugs or short wide vases can be used for holding wooden spoons, cooking utensils, paint brushes, or makeup brushes. Blanket storage boxes can be used for storing winter sweaters and sporting gear.

Dividers Cutlery dividers can be used to sort makeup and beauty supplies in bathroom drawers. Dividers in a clothing drawer can keep socks from undies. Also consider cupboard dividers that might create half shelves. In a kitchen cabinet, a half-shelf divider can be very useful in organizing spices for easy accessibility—or you might consider a drawer divider designed for just that use. A vertical divider in the cupboard over a refrigerator can be a useful device for sorting trays. In a bureau, armoire, or bedroom cupboard, stacking dividers can be used for separating various items of clothing or bed and bath linens.

Shelves Think of shelves as being capable of holding and organizing far more than books. A shelf over your washer and dryer can be used for holding all of your laundry products. A kitchen shelf can hold a collection of teapots or cookbooks, freeing up cupboard and counter space. Shelving in a closet provides a useful means of organizing shoes, purses, and hats. A bathroom shelf can hold a stack of towels.

Wall Units A Peg-board with hooks is an excellent device in a child's room for organizing coats, umbrellas, hats. In a kitchen, some types of racks can be used for suspending pots, pans, or for hanging mugs and cooking utensils.

Specialty Units Various types of shoe trees or shoe bags can be placed on the backs of closet doors. A wide variety of items termed "organizers," valets, caddies, or racks are available.

Clustering Hints

- Use only one container per type of item. Have one container for all your spools of thread, not five.

- Use items you already have. Chances are, you already have enough boxes, bins, and baskets to put more than half of your unorganized possessions into order.

- When buying additional storage items, look for durability, adjustability, and stackability.

Remember: a place for everything and everything in its place. Get items grouped together. And keep those items grouped together. Teach your children at an early age that when they are finished using an item, they must put it back in its place. Develop that habit yourself.

11 ✔ Designating Spaces

The second step related to clustering is to designate spaces for certain activities. Every home tends to need these four designated spaces:

A Place for Arrival   Every house or apartment has a main entrance for family use. Within that area, you need a place to dump what you bring in from the outside world, whether it's a briefcase, an arm load of grocery sacks, or a dripping umbrella. Consider the old-fashioned back porch. It had many features still needed today by virtually all families.

- A place to clean your shoes, or remove your shoes. A washable floor mat and a shoe rack can help keep the rest of your house cleaner.

- A place to hang a wet garment or stash a wet umbrella. Umbrella stands and plastic-coated peg racks are good ideas.

- A table for temporarily placing what is in your hands. This table can also be used for items that need to be taken out, such as school lunch pails.

- A bin for wet or soiled garments.

- A bin or basket for depositing trash brought in from outside, or your car.

- A paper towel rack for your ready use in dealing with spills or messes best left on the porch and not brought into the rest of the house.

Let your "arrival spot" become your first line of defense for organizing and ordering your gear.

A Place to Eat For as many meals as possible, limit your family's dining to a specific place, such as the kitchen counter or table. Not only will cleaning up after meals be easier, but you'll avoid messy spills in other areas of the house that take time, and sometimes money, to clean.

A Place for Projects Have a designated space for sewing, craft projects, and hobbies, preferably a room or area of a room with a large work surface. Limit the number of projects that can be ongoing at any one time, and also limit the amount of time the work space can be occupied by that project. If you don't place limitations on the work space, you might find that you have a doll house under construction in the corner of the kitchen for six months, or that every room of the house has a craft project in progress.

A Place to Play Every room in your house need not be considered a playroom. Limit your child to a specific room for play, and insist that each game or toy be put away promptly when the child is finished with it. You'll save yourself a lot of headaches and hassle if you help your children develop the habit of putting away one toy or game before moving on to a new one.

12 ✔ Designating Places

You'll save yourself hours of roaming your home or rummaging through pockets and purses if you have designated places for these three must-have-right-now items:

Keys Install a key rack in your kitchen or porch area, a place where you can keep all the keys of all family members. Get in the habit of putting your keys there as soon as you walk in the door.

Limit yourself to one set of keys that you take with you from home to work or on errands, and back. Include in that set all of the keys that you need on a daily or regular basis. Keep other keys, which are used only periodically, on separate rings. Label every set of keys.

Should you find that you are frequently locking yourself out of your home or car, keep a second set of keys on your car (such as in a magnetized holder that can be hidden in the engine area or under the frame) or at your home (perhaps under a specified rock or taped to the underside of a planter).

Eyeglasses or Contact Lenses Have a designated place for your reading glasses, sunglasses, and your spare pair of glasses or contact lenses. When you take off a pair of glasses, put them immediately in the place you have designated. Choose a place that protects your eyewear. If you travel a great deal, have a place for putting your extra eyeware (in a briefcase, suitcase, or the glove compartment of your car). Make sure you have sturdy eyewear holders.

Hearing Aids and Dentures When you remove your hearing aid or dentures, immediately put them in a designated space—one in which they will not only be safe, but remain clean.

Other Quick-Access Items Several other items also seem to call for a designated place of their own. *Pocket change:* a small coin purse can be a valuable item to tuck into the glove compartment of your car; refill it periodically with change from your wallet so that you will always have money for parking meters or tolls. *Car registration and proof of insurance:* have a designated place within your car for holding your car registration and proof of insurance. *Claim tickets:* have a special place for all of your claim checks; that way, when you get ready to go pick up the items you've taken in for service or processing, you'll be able to find the stubs you need quickly and easily.

13 ✔ Cleaning Out

As you begin to cluster items together, set up five containers labeled as follows:

- *Throw away.* You can use your normal trash bin for this one.

- *Give away.* A big, sturdy box or two will probably suffice. You may want to have one box for specific give-aways (to relatives or friends), and one box for charity donations.

- *Recycle.* You may need several sacks or boxes for this area—one each for glass, plastic, paper, and aluminum.

- *Repair.* Make certain that items you put into this pile are ones you want to keep, items that can be repaired, and items that are cost-effective to repair (as opposed to buying a new item). A word of caution about repair containers. They can remain filled for a long time, and become just another box or basket of clutter. Make a deal with yourself that if an item remains in a repair container for longer than three months, you'll shift it over to the throw-away container.

- *Return.* When you begin a serious effort at bringing order to your home or apartment, you'll probably be amazed at how many items you have that are borrowed and need to be returned. Label each item with a strip of masking tape, indicating to whom it belongs, and put yourself on a schedule for returning the things that aren't yours.

As each container becomes full, deal with it. If it's trash, put it out for collection. If it's for charity, seal up the box and deliver it. If it's recyclable, bag it, put it into the trunk of your car, and drive to the depository.

Four Key Questions to Ask   As you begin to cluster a particular category or possession, evaluate each item before it goes into its new container. Ask yourself these four questions:

- Have I used this in the past two years?

- Can I anticipate a specific time (function, event, or reason) to use this within the next two years?

- Does this item give me aesthetic pleasure?

- Does this item have value as an heirloom, or am I saving it for a specific person? (Be sure you can name the person to whom you expect to give the item.)

Unless you can answer yes to at least one of these questions, discard the item and don't think twice about it. Face up to the fact that you probably never will need it. And no, it probably won't be worth a lot of money someday. No matter what you paid for the item initially, if you aren't using it, don't derive aesthetic pleasure from it, or don't consider it to be of heirloom value, there's really no reason for you to keep it. Give it to someone who can use it or who will enjoy it.

Clutter-Elimination Motivators   The best motivator for removing clutter is to work at the task with others. Provide a means of rewarding yourself or family for getting rid of the clutter. You might set up a scale and record the number of pounds of stuff you give away, throw away, or otherwise eliminate. Set up a reward system in advance according to the number of pounds you eliminate—perhaps a family outing to a movie, beach, or concert.

Keep your eyes focused clearly on the goal: eliminating excess in order to have more access to the things that you truly use, need, and enjoy having around.

14 ✔ Clothing Control

We tend not to wear or use things we don't see, so the number-one principle in organizing a closet is this: have all items in full view.

Use shoe boxes that are clear, or remove the ends of cardboard boxes and stack them. Use shoe bags for holding stockings, scarves, gloves, or rolled-up belts. Add enough storage bins or shelving so that you can readily see your folded sweaters, hats, and purses.

Divide and Conquer Get organized by dividing your clothing in these four ways:

- Separate your nonclothing items from your clothing, and remove all nonclothing items from your closet or drawers.

- Separate your closet and drawer space into your space and any space you may share with a spouse, roommate, or sibling.

- Separate your in-season clothing from out-of-season clothing. Put the in-season clothing at the front of your closet or drawer space. As the seasons change, move appropriate garments into the up-front position.

- Separate clothing by type: formal and casual. Hang coordinating elements within close proximity. You may find that you are visually able to put together looks that you didn't realize you were capable of creating.

Twice a year, or at the change of seasons, reevaluate your clothing. If an item is worn or faded beyond repair or use, discard it. If you haven't worn the item in the past two years or if the item has outlived its style, give it away.

Realize that garments need space in order to breathe. Your clothes will last longer, smell better, and require less cleaning and ironing if you give each garment enough room to hang freely.

Repair-and-Clean Basket When you find an item of clothing that needs repair or cleaning, separate it immediately from your other garments and put it in a designated laundry basket. Then take those items to the cleaners or shoe repair shop as soon as possible. If an item needs hemming or mending, deal with it as quickly as you can schedule a repair hour. You'll save yourself a great deal of frustration if you keep the garments in your wardrobe ready to wear.

15 ✔ Pantry and Cupboard Control

You can apply to your kitchen many of the same techniques you have used to bring order to your wardrobe.

Kitchen cupboards have a way of harboring little-used or outdated items, from small appliances to old spices. Ask yourself about appliances:

- Have I used this item in the last year?

- Can I think of a specific time I will use it during the coming six months?

If your answer is no to both questions, that item should go out the door. Also ask yourself, "How many of this item do I have?" You may be surprised to find that you have more than one potato masher or cheese grater, or that you have three jars of cumin powder among your spices. If you have excess, get rid of it.

In bringing order to kitchen cupboards, the rule of thumb is this: if you can't reach it, you won't use it. Bring into easy reach all the items that you need or use on a regular basis. You should be able to reach within one or two steps all you need to prepare an average meal.

Hard-to-Reach Areas
Reserve the top shelves of your cupboards for dishes and glassware you only use on special occasions. You can also stash your unused extras on the top shelves; for example, if you have twelve plates but use four of them, keep four on a lower shelf, and put the other eight on the top shelf. Consider a half-shelf divider and use the extra space for the bowls or glasses you use most often.

Storage for Perishables
Make certain you have sufficient storage containers for items that need to be kept airtight or sealed. Choose see-through containers that are stackable. Cannister lids should fit tightly.

Five Basic Tips
Here are five tips for saving time and effort, and for bringing order to kitchen disorder:

- *Keep your work surface as clear as possible.* If you have to remove items from a counter-top or table before you can use it, find another place for those items.

- *Clean up as you go.* Don't let the dishes pile high. Rinse them and put them into the dishwasher before the food has time to stick.

- *Use a dishwasher-safe spoon rest or small tray for tea bags and cooking spoons and utensils.*

- *Cluster items.* Keep your canned goods together. Cluster the items you need for baking, and cluster the utensils you use when baking. Stack items that come in floppy pouches, such as beans, soup mixes, and dried foods, or toss them into a stackable bin in a pantry area.

- *Think in terms of cubic space in your cupboards and under your cupboards.* Use shelf dividers and stacking units. Hang cups and mugs from the underside of cupboard shelves. If counter space is a premium, consider appliances that attach to the bottom of cabinets.

Safety First   Make certain that kitchen cleansers, bug sprays, and other poisonous items are kept out of reach of young children. Toddler-proof your lower cupboards and drawers with safety latches. Keep the trash can away from curious toddlers. Consider installing burn-guards for your stove top. Make certain that you have a fire extinguisher within easy access to your stove—but out of the reach of young children—and that you know how to use it.

16 ✔ A Place for Tools and Equipment

The three tools most frequently used by most people are few in number and very simple to store: a hammer, a screwdriver, and a pair of pliers. If these and a few other simple devices (tape measure, level, and wire cutters) are all you have, you can easily store these items in a shoe box that's clearly labeled. Unfortunately, most of us have a tool collection that goes far beyond these basics!

You may want to designate a drawer for the small items that we all seem to need periodically, such as batteries, picture hangers, and spare fuses. Most other tools can be stored in a garage or area over a workbench using a Peg-board and hooks.

If you need space for tools and don't have a garage or extra closet space, you may want to consider buying a footlocker or trunk (one you can lock). Such an item can be used as a coffee table, be covered with a fabric skirt and become a "specialty" table, or simply be stashed in the corner of a room as a decorative item. Guests need never guess the contents!

Yard and Garden Equipment In storing yard and garden equipment, make certain the equipment is not accessible to young children. Gasoline and other types of fuels, as well as insecticides, gardening supplies, fertilizers, and de-icing agents should be stored properly. Cluster these items together on shelves. A locked cabinet can be a useful unit for storing small equipment and garden supplies in a garage.

Bicycles Use racks in your garage to store bicycles. A bicycle that is hung, suspended, or kept vertical takes up less space than one that is laid on its side. Cluster items required for bike repair and equipment used for biking safety.

MONEY CONTROL

Four specific ways to put more
order into your finances

17 ✔ Shop Specifically

"Just browsing" generally translates into wasted money, unfocused time, and unwanted possessions. Impulse buying does more to torpedo a carefully plotted financial plan than any other single action over which you can exert control. Here are four strategies for helping you avoid the gotta-have-it-right-now syndrome:

Shop with Lists Make a written list before you shop, and discipline yourself to stick to the list. This principle applies to all purchases, not just groceries. Keep tucked into your purse three ongoing lists:

- *The year-round-gift-shopping list.* On this list, have the names of people you anticipate "gifting" during the holiday season, or for birthdays, anniversaries, or other special occasions. (Ideally, next to each name you have put a dollar figure based on the annualized budget you prepared in chapter 1.) Should you see an item that you think is a perfect gift for a person for a specific occasion, check your list to make certain that you haven't already purchased something for that person, check the price against your proposed budget for both the gift and the amount you intended to spend that month on gifts, and if all signals are green, go for it.

- *The wardrobe-needs list.* As you have organized your clothing in chapter 14, and have reevaluated your wardrobe needs each season, you have discovered some gaps in your wardrobe that you'd like to fill. Those needs can be subjected to the same process as purchasing a gift. Does it fit your need, your budget?

- *The waiting-for-it-to-go-on-sale list.* Think through the things you find yourself purchasing year after year—from holiday greeting cards to garden fertilizer. Make a list of them. Then attempt to purchase these items when they go on sale.

Avoid the Unexpected "Discount" Temptation

Many times we see items on sale and find the savings irresistible. Rather than look at the savings, look at the remaining dollar figure. Is the item something you really need? Is the money for this item in your budget? No matter how good the bargain, if you don't need the item right away or can't afford it, it's not a good purchase. The same goes for coupons. Even if the manufacturer offers you a dollar off, if the item isn't one you use or need, why spend $4 to save $1?

Shop with a Dollar Limit and Take Cash
You can avoid the tendency to splurge or purchase on impulse by consulting your budget before you go shopping, and setting a dollar limit on the amount you will spend for that particular outing. Then take just that much cash with you and leave all your credit cards at home. You'll find it more difficult to part with cash or to write a check than to spend "plastic money," and those extra few moments of hesitation may give you just the time you need to rethink an impulsive decision.

Avoid Shopping in "Clutter Traps"
Avoid those places that cry out to you to purchase items that you are going to call *clutter* six months from now. These include souvenir shops or garage sales and flea markets. If you are collecting a specific type of object or are seeking to complete an antique set of china or silver, be sure you take a specific list with you and refuse to be tempted by anything else.

18 ✔ Research Your Major Purchases

Major purchases can range from an appliance to a piece of furniture to a vehicle to a new fall suit. The definition of *major* is up to you. A new coffeemaker or a new toaster may be a purchase well worth a little research.

Begin Your Research at Home Start your purchasing research at home. Before going out to shop for back-to-school clothes, take a look at what still fits each child, what might be passed down from one child to the next, and what can be updated with new accessories. Make a list of what you *have,* rather than what you *need.*

In preparing for the purchase of an appliance or piece of furniture measure the space where you anticipate placing the item. (No need to shop for a baby grand piano if you only have room for an upright!) Ask what best suits your needs.

Consult the Experts Look through magazines to get ideas about ways in which you might fit a new purchase into your existing environment. Keep in mind that the rooms pictured in magazines are likely to be bigger than those in your home or apartment.

Consider the performance level of an item. Has the item been evaluated by a magazine that compares and rates products? Take time to visit your public library and read these reviews.

Consider your friends and associates to be user-friendly and user-wise experts. Ask what they have purchased and how satisfied they are.

Ask Questions of the Salesman How does this model compare to other models or brands? Have you had any of these items returned? Why? What warranty is included? Where can the item be serviced? Think in terms of performance first; from among those near-equals, choose the style you like.

Try It Out Just as you'd try on a coat before buying it, try out an appliance or take a vehicle for a test drive before you make a decision. Don't let the salesman push the vacuum cleaner on the showroom floor carpet; *you* push it. Does it feel right to *you*? Can you maneuver it easily? Can you attach the accessories easily? Lie down on the mattress. Sit on the sofa.

Comparison Shop Don't fall victim to the first salesman you encounter. Even after carefully conducting your home and expert research, make a commitment to evaluating—on site—at least three different brands or models, preferably in three different stores.

19 ✔ Buy Quality

A better quality item will probably last longer and provide more satisfaction than an item of less quality. Style and brand name may or may not be equated with quality; a high price tag doesn't ensure it. Quality is generally based on these factors:

- *Material used in construction.* Are you dealing with hardwood or fiberboard? What type of stuffing has been used? What is the spring construction? How much steel has been used? Is the fabric tightly or loosely woven?

- *Sturdiness of construction.* Are the joints of a piece of furniture notched together or glued? Are the seams tightly stitched?

- *Durability or life expectancy.* How long does the manufacturer expect the item to last? In the experience of your friends, experts, and even the salesman, how long does the item actually last?

- *Smoothness of operation.* Do the working parts fit together well and run smoothly?

Ask about the number of working parts; the fewer the parts, the less chance of breakage.

* *Manufacturer's reliability.* Find out who manufactures the item you are seeking to buy. What is their reputation for quality in the industry?

New or Used

Quality isn't necessarily dependent on the age of an item. A better gauge is the amount of use against the total life expectancy of the item. A luxury car that is two years old and has been well maintained may be a much wiser, more cost-effective purchase than a new economy car.

The Wise-Purchase Rule

A simple purchasing rule to keep in mind is this: *Purchase the greatest amount of quality that you can within your budget.* In purchasing quality, you are likely to find yourself reducing quantity. Fewer items of better quality tend to equal less clutter, wiser use of money, savings in time, and a lot more pleasure in a purchase.

20 ✔ Keep Track of Your Money

Many of us end up with too much month at the end of our paycheck. Here are some ways to track where your money is spent:

- *Set up a simple ledger system for keeping track of your money.* Include both income and expenses. An expense ledger is a "clustering" activity. Record income and expenses according to different categories of purchase. Your ledger will generally have the same categories as your budget.

- *Save every receipt and record every purchase.* If you don't get a receipt with a purchase, make a note on a scrap of paper. Periodically, record your purchases in a ledger. Divide your ledger according to categories: mortgage, food, clothing, yard care, medical, and so forth. You may have as many as twenty to thirty categories. If the purchase isn't tax deductible, or if you don't need to compare the receipt to a monthly statement, toss it after recording the amount.

  At the end of each month, tally up your

purchases in any given category and compare them to your budget. Where have you gone over or under budget? By comparing your actual expenses against your budget, you can keep your overall financial picture in order. It's easier to put on the brakes of your spending if you catch yourself speeding before going too far down the road.

- *Balance your bank accounts monthly.* Do this without fail. You'll save yourself overdraft charges, and have a feeling of greater control over your finances. If you have made a math error, it's better to catch it within a matter of days than to let it go on for months.

- *Keep a tax record box or file.* As you record your expenses, put receipts related to taxes in a separate file. Put your bank statements and completed check registers in a box; at year's end, your detailed ledger, tax file, and banking box should provide you with all of the information you need for fairly quick and easy preparation of your tax forms.

TIME CONTROL

Fifteen suggestions for making
the most of your time

21 ✔ Plan Your Day

An unplanned day isn't likely to be as productive as a planned one. And, productive days tend to be ones that give more joy and a greater sense of purpose.

Live a Day at a Time   Take each day as a separate unit. Attempt to do in a day all that you can do, and then move on to the next day. Don't live in the past, or you'll always feel as if you are playing catch-up. If you live in the future, you'll probably never arrive where or when you thought you would. Limit your scope to the sixteen or so waking hours that are immediately ahead of you.

List Tomorrow's Activities at the Close of Today   Make a list before you go to bed of all the things you want to do during the upcoming day. After listing the things you want to do, survey your list. Have you put down too many things for one day? What can you drop off the list? Don't overbook yourself.

If you could only do one thing on tomorrow's list, what would it be? Give that item the priority spot. Then rank other activities in decreasing order of importance. Consider what the optimum time for you to engage in each activity might be. Use your most productive hours for tasks that require your best effort. Schedule appointments during your less productive hours.

Identify Time Wasters   Isolate those events in your daily routine that eat up time without giving you much reward. Try to eliminate them, or cut down on their number, frequency, and time allotment. The same goes for interruptions; learn to say no to events or activities.

Schedule Alone Time   Be sure to include some time on your schedule every day in which you can be alone, to do what you want to do. You need to have a little time you can call your own— for meditation, prayer, or just a little bit of distance from the hectic swirl of the world. Your day will feel as if you have more order and balance to it if you'll schedule at least a half hour for yourself.

22 ✔ Delegate

If you find more things on a daily list than you can handle successfully, you have three choices: (1) do each task halfway (and feel frustrated, disappointed, and stressed); (2) don't do a task at all; (3) solicit help. This last is the best option, and one that actually provides an opportunity for relationships, joy, and greater balance in your life.

- *Determine precisely what it is that you want the other person to do.* The whole task? Part of the task? Intermittently? All the time? On a schedule? On a rotation with others? If you are soliciting help from a superior, be able to state why you need help and exactly what form you would like the help to take. Be able to state your request in clear, concise terms, and ask the other person to reiterate their new responsibilities to you. Ask, rather than demand.

- *How much supervision will you give the other person who is helping?* Continuous? (If so, you haven't truly delegated.) Periodic? None? Delegating doesn't mean abdicating;

it does mean that you accept ultimate responsibility for the task, but that you are giving the majority of that responsibility to another person.

All Hands on Deck   No one is too young to help around the house; have something for everybody to do. Chores shouldn't be an option for children; they should be a part of life's routine.

Keep in mind that nothing is ever done perfectly, even by you! Relax and compromise. If you don't, you probably won't enjoy the time you have freed up by delegating.

Share the Reward   You'll be gaining a reward through delegating: valuable time. Make sure the person to whom you have delegated a task is also rewarded in some way.

23 ✔ Take Time to Do It Right

A job done halfway is a job that is likely to need redoing. A job done halfheartedly is likely to be a job that brings no sense of satisfaction, fulfillment, or joy.

If you agree to undertake a task or relationship, put your best effort into it. That includes giving the task or relationship sufficient time.

Sufficient Time Sufficient time has two dimensions: quality and quantity. The quality of a time segment is usually directly related to these three factors:

- *Focus.* Is the time being devoted exclusively to one task, one person, one topic? To have quality time, you need to eliminate all distractions.

- *Shared Meaning.* All persons involved must regard the time as valuable and important.

- *Satisfaction.* When the time segment is over, all parties involved should feel a sense of satisfaction, resolve, accomplishment, forward motion, release. There should be a sense that something has been shared, enjoyed, experienced, given, or received.

The quantity of a time segment requires that you make certain you have given yourself enough time to do or contribute your best. Doing your best doesn't mean demanding perfection from yourself or others. There's a balance between attempting to do excellent work and doing perfect work. Perfection generally requires more time and money than can be regained or justified.

Time Axioms Keep in mind these two key principles about time. *You never arrive if you don't get started.* Avoid the tendency to procrastinate. Jump into projects with both feet, and a lot of enthusiasm. The only way you can ever have sufficient time for a project is if you begin immediately; otherwise, you'll always feel behind and scrambling to make a deadline.

The longer and more frequent the time segments you allocate to something, the more you'll build momentum. Even though you may break a major project down into segments, cluster the segments together and work to build a sense of forward motion.

24 ✔ Schedule Maintenance

Every aspect of your life requires maintenance: your health, home, vehicle, relationships, career, faith, finances. To maintain involves repairing, refurbishing, replacing, restoring, renewing, realigning, rebuilding. The important news about maintenance is that it saves both time and money in the long run. The good news about maintenance is that it can be scheduled. You have control over when, where, and how maintenance takes place.

On an annual basis, schedule key maintenance days. Put them in red on a calendar and consider them appointments that can't be adjusted except in emergency situations. Include the following:

- *An annual physical exam* for yourself and for each child.

- *Annual or semiannual visits to medical specialists* who are helping you manage long-term health, such as your dentist, optometrist, dermatologist.

- *A meeting with your financial adviser, accountant, or tax attorney.* Do this at the beginning of the third quarter of your fiscal year. That way, you will still have time to make some adjustments within your fiscal year, and at the same time, get a running start on planning your financial strategy for the coming year.

- *Any meetings you anticipate needing with other key professionals, associates, or clients,* such as your attorney, stock broker, insurance agent, key staff members or colleagues, or major clients.

- *Maintenance on your heating and air conditioning units* prior to the season in which they will be needed most.

- *A maintenance-review day for your house and yard.* Are there trees that need to be trimmed or removed? Shingles that need to be replaced?

- *A time for a spiritual retreat,* perhaps a day, weekend, or week, either to be alone, with your spouse, with your family, or with others of like faith.

- *A time for a family vacation,* with major emphasis on recreation, relaxation, and renewal.

- *A time of learning, mental and creative stimulation, growth*—perhaps a short course, a special series of lectures or concerts, a set of lessons, or a seminar.

• *Vehicle maintenance.* Consult the odometer on each vehicle you own, and estimate when you will need to take the vehicle in for maintenance, as recommended in your owner's manual. Include as vehicle maintenance the renewal of licenses.

Remind Yourself to Make Appointments
Prior to key dates on your calendar, remind yourself to make appointments. For example, a couple of months prior to the date you've designated for your physical exam, write a little note on your calendar: "Call today for annual physical date. See March 23."

Keep Your Maintenance Dates
Don't shove maintenance to the side because something better or more important pops up. If you must readjust a date, make sure you don't eliminate the maintenance appointment. Reschedule it as soon as possible.

25 ✔ Hire Professionals When You Need Them

You may be *able* to do it yourself, but not want to spend the time; you may *not* be able to do it yourself. Either way, if you hire it done, choose a professional. This person has done the job before, has a track record of good performance, and is willing to supply you with references.

Check references before making a final decision. Ask if the person is willing to sign a performance agreement, a statement guaranteeing his or her work, or a document that outlines mutual expectations. A true professional will stand by his or her work.

Get an estimate. A true professional will not only be able to supply you with a written estimate or a statement of hourly fees, but will consider it a normal part of doing business. Professional help may cost a little more than doing the job yourself. But, in the long run, professional help is likely to be cost effective in terms of time.

Balancing Time and Money   As you weigh the need for professional services, here are some questions to ask.

- *If I Do It.* Can I do this task? Can I do it as well as a professional? How long would it take me to do it? Will I need to buy any special tools or equipment that I don't already have? How much will my doing this disrupt our normal family routine or schedule? Will I enjoy doing it? Will my family enjoy my doing it, or enjoy helping?

- *If They Do It.* How much more will it cost for me to have this job done by a professional? Will that person be able to save me money in some way? Will they be able to do this job in a way that brings less disruption to my sense of personal or family balance?

- *Who Will Do It?* If the trade-off comes down to time or money, which would I rather have? If I choose time, will I consider the money well-spent?

26 ✔ Once-a-Month Errands

Ever hear of the days when folks only went to town once a month? That principle can still work for you, to time-saving advantage.

The Errand Basket During my growing-up years, my mother had a small basket in her home office in which she put little slips of paper, each with a specific errand or purchase that she anticipated making the next time we went to the city, which was twenty miles away. When errand day arrived, Mom went through her slips of paper, gathering together various items and sorting them geographically. Off we went. As each errand was completed, we'd tear up the slip and toss it into the litter caddy. If the errand couldn't be accomplished for some reason, we put the slip of paper to the bottom of the pile and returned it to the basket once we got home. It was a game, of sorts, for us to see what all we might accomplish in six hours of running city errands, with only one round trip's worth of gasoline and time.

I still follow that example, which I share with my own children in these words: Let's not venture out to the mall until we have sufficient reason to go.

27 ✔ Map Out Errand Runs

In gathering errands and lists together for periodic shopping excursions, you'll find that you can save a great deal of time by clustering your errands according to the following:

Geographic Location Map out a route for your errands. While in an area of town, or an area of the mall, do everything there that you need to do. If you have older children or teens who are going along, you may want to give them the challenge of figuring out the best way to go.

As you anticipate going into a well-frequented grocery or department store, map out a strategy in your own mind for getting all of the items on your list in the least amount of time. You may enjoy walking up and down each aisle occasionally, but you don't need to go up and down every aisle on every trip.

Time of Day Try to get to the busiest or most popular store on your agenda as it opens. You'll get a better parking spot, better service, and save minutes in the process. If you need to drop off an item for repair, evaluation, or processing, plan to make those stops among your first ones of the day.

End your errands and head for home before rush hour traffic; or plan to have supper out as a treat at the close of your errand run, and return home after the rush hour. Hours spent idling on a freeway are wasted.

Divide and Shop   Older children and teenagers will enjoy having time to shop on their own. Synchronize your watches, set a meeting time and location, and go your separate ways. You might insist that your child stay within the same store, or same department, or even within sight. You might insist that your children stay together as a group. You'll all enjoy the outing, and you'll be helping to develop a sense of responsibility in your child.

Running Errands with Children   Discuss with your children what you are hoping to buy or do, what it is that you are looking for, and why. Try to beat your own schedule. Laugh a lot as you go. And stop occasionally to teach your child about the objects you encounter along the way, or about how to conduct certain business transactions. The time together will become both quality and quantity time, not just errand-running time!

28 ✔ Cluster Appointments

If you are going to take part of a day off for a doctor's appointment, you might as well take the rest of the day off for an eye exam, or an appointment with your attorney. Make a personal day off really count. It may not seem like a true vacation day, but it's likely to be a satisfying day of accomplishment, a day that restores a sense of balance and control, and a day that provides a change of pace.

Choose professionals who will help you stick to your schedule. You shouldn't have to wait in a doctor's or dentist's office more than twenty minutes. If you do, talk to your physician about the wait. Ask if there's a better time of day for you to make an appointment so that you can both stay on schedule. Let the professional know that you value his or her time and expertise greatly, but that you also value your own time.

Family Appointments If you are making an appointment for your child to see the family dentist, make back-to-back appointments for all your children. Better to spend an hour at the dentist and have all three children see the dentist than to spend an hour coming and going from each of three appointments. The same can go for back-to-school physicals, eye appointments, and shoe shopping.

Group Training If there's a new skill to be learned, gather everyone together for a one-time explanation or training session. The task need not be a major one; it might be instruction on how to use the new phone system or how to attach and use the new lawn sprinkler.

29 ✔ Use the Phone

Don't drive—dial. A phone call can accomplish a great deal. Even a brief call can help you remember a birthday or other special occasion, maintain a relationship across a great distance, get information on the price, availability, or specifications of a product, service, or event, get directions, or place an order. As an added bonus, you can shop, gather information, exchange opinions, make decisions, and conduct meetings by phone without giving a second thought to your own physical appearance.

Good Phone Use   Use the phone with your intended purpose in mind. If you get a machine, leave a message. If all you intended to do with the call was convey a piece of information, don't invite a return call.

Use your own answering machine to screen calls. In your answering machine message, ask for as much information as possible. Try to avoid having to return calls only to get a needed fact or two.

Establish a Phone Time in Your Work Day   Use low-energy hours for making and returning phone calls. Invite others to call you during that same time. Let it be known that your mornings are for creative work or intense project development, and that you receive and return calls in the afternoon.

The Advantage of Portable and Speaker Phones   Cordless phones, cellular phones, and even phones with speakers or extra long cords, can give you a great deal of mobility and allow you to talk even as you engage in another activity.

30 ✔ Establish a Daily Household Routine

Put your household on a schedule and you'll not only save time, but you'll actually become more spontaneous. Here's how.

Create a Family Routine Establish a set pattern of times for going to bed and getting up. This can vary from person to person, but make certain that each person has a schedule of sleep which becomes a norm. Without sufficient regular patterns of sleep, the rest of a day's schedule is difficult to set or maintain.

Based on getting-up times and bedtimes, establish times for a family breakfast and dinner. Give yourself enough time to enjoy these meals together as a family. Even if you only carve out fifteen minutes to sit down together for each meal, you'll benefit by having this time together to share your lives, to plan your days, to discuss your tragedies, triumphs, and trials, to share opinions and insights, to exchange news, to bring up questions. Set times for:

- *Chores.* If you want the trash taken out in the morning, put it on the schedule. If you want the bed made before the child has breakfast, set up the routine that way.

- *Homework.* The time for homework may be right after school, right after dinner, or a few minutes in the morning before school. Set aside a place and time for quiet concentration.

- *Practice.* If you have more than one child needing to put in practice time on the family piano, schedule it.

- *Bathtime.* If you have more than two people sharing a bathroom, you'll need to come up with a schedule—showers in the morning for some, baths at night for others.

Where's the Spontaneity?

Every hour that isn't scheduled or every minute that is created when a task is completed satisfactorily ahead of schedule becomes a moment for fun. Free time becomes the goal and the reward. This approach helps a child set priorities and become self-motivating and self-rewarding.

A family with a routine is a family that has an overall sense of order. In the process, you'll be teaching your children principles of time management that can last an entire lifetime.

31 ✔ Avoid the Crunch of Holiday Shopping

You can save a great deal of time and money by planning your gift-giving on an annual basis and making purchases all through the year. Include birthday, anniversary, and graduation gifts on your annual list.

You'll save time by avoiding holiday traffic, busy shopping centers, and long lines. You'll save money by taking advantage of sales, and by budgeting your giving dollars as a hedge against impulse buying and last-minute overspending.

Have a Gift Drawer or Trunk Have a place you can designate as a gift container, and use it for stashing gifts as you purchase them throughout the year. You can help ensure the secrecy of your gifts by wrapping them immediately after their purchase.

You will want to carry your master gift list with you at all times. Be sure to include a couple of all-purpose gifts on your annual list, such as candles, sachets, gift soaps, or specialty tea bags. That way, you'll never need to rush out for a last-minute gift. Should an unexpected guest arrive during a holiday celebration, you'll be able to present a gift with just a few minutes of preparation.

Gift-Giving Supplies Cluster all of your gift-wrapping supplies, including wrapping and tissue paper, ribbons and bows. Buy your supplies during sales, the best of which usually occur in late December or early January.

32 ✔ Enlist Your Friends as Scouts

Do you want to locate a hard-to-find item, a certain antique pattern, a scarf or accessory with specific colors, a great buy on a specific model of appliance or piece of furniture? Ask your friends to keep their eyes open on your behalf.

Shopping Savvy You certainly can't explore every store or contact every supplier of an item in your area. And bargains and distinctive items are sometimes found in the least likely places.

Virtually everyone has at least one or more friends who love to shop. They'll probably be delighted to help you out; in fact, they'll probably find great satisfaction in looking on your behalf. (It gives them an excuse to explore new stores or to justify time spent browsing.)

Friendly Advice Sometimes friends or acquaintances are actually quite experienced or knowledgeable about a particular item. For example, you may have a friend who is a real car nut—a person who is frequently trading in cars, making deals, scouting out the showrooms, test-driving new models, talking about various vehicles.

Ask that friend's advice as you do research on the purchase of a new vehicle for yourself. They'll be able to tell you a great deal that you won't have gained from other sources. Then, if you narrow your choice to a particular model or two, you might ask the person again for their opinion, or ask where they think you can get the best price or deal.

33 ✔ Redeem the Spare Minutes

Everybody has a few spare minutes in every day. Give some order and fulfillment to this time by finding innovative uses for it.

Here are things you can do that take only a few minutes—time you might have while waiting for the children to emerge from school, for your appointment to arrive, for your plane to begin boarding:

- Write out a list

- Balance your checkbook

- Clean out your purse

- Read a passage from the Bible

- Do some isometric exercises

- Skim through a magazine, journal article, or report

- List your expenses on an expense-account form

- Memorize a verse of Scripture or the stanza of a poem

Items to Have with You Always   There are items I carry with me virtually everywhere. They all fit very easily in a briefcase or large purse or tote. As a result, I always have plenty to do, even if I only have five or ten minutes of time. These include: *my master calendar,* which includes my lists, address book, several cards with envelopes, stamps for both postcards and letters, and blank notepaper for making lists, *a purse-size copy of the Bible, my checkbook register, magazine articles,* or *a paperback book* I want to read, and *a small tape recorder and three tapes* (one of inspiration or education, one of music, and one blank, for recording my own ideas).

Information on the Go   Consider using commuting time to learn a new skill, a new language, or listen to a new novel or self-help lecture. Numerous audiocassette programs are available for check-out through public libraries. Your friends may also be willing to loan you a set of seminar tapes, a novel on tape, or other materials they have purchased or acquired. Turn your car or train into a moving continuing-education center.

Fitness for Body and Mind   You can also use a Walkman or cassette player to add to your storehouse of knowledge while you walk or jog, ride an exercise bike, or use a rowing machine.

34 ✔ Landscape with Time in Mind

Unless gardening and yard upkeep are your passions, you may find that the ground around your house yields more burden than joy. If that's the case, you have two options:

Hire It Done If you choose this route, hire reliable experts whom you don't need to supervise closely, and work out a payment plan that doesn't require your presence while the work is being done.

Simplify the Process Choose plants and trees that require minimal care. Evergreens have a lot going for them! Consider adding more beds for shrubs and flowering bushes, reducing the square yards of grass that need to be mowed, weeded, fertilized, and watered. Once planted, a bed with a few large shrubs and a thick layer of bark covering the ground requires far less care than grass.

Create patios and other areas that can be swept or washed off easily. Consider limiting your annual flowers to a few beds or pots. Choose plants that are suited for your geographic area, and that grow with minimal pruning, spraying, fertilizing, or fumigating.

If you have two green thumbs and you love to putter in the garden, if you enjoy the pleasures of home-grown vegetables, fruits, and flowers, or if you derive benefit from sweating out your frustrations as you mow the yard, then design your yard to give you the pleasures you enjoy. The time a complicated yard takes probably won't seem wasted or burdensome to you.

What goes for yards can also apply to house plants or pots of flowers and vegetables on a patio or balcony in an apartment complex. Unless you enjoy having living plants around, don't feel compelled to have them.

If you have young children, landscape with their safety in mind. Avoid using chemicals on your lawn. Don't plant bushes that produce poisonous berries. Keep areas clear for play.

35 ✔ The Night Before

Even the most energetic "morning" person should make good use of the last hour of the preceding day. During the final hour before you begin preparing for bed, make your list of things to do the upcoming day and prioritize your agenda.

Get out the garments you plan to wear, as well as the garments, socks, and shoes for each of your children. Also put out any accessories, such as belts, hair ribbons, ties, or jewelry.

Load up your briefcase or tote bag with the things you anticipate taking with you through the day. Make certain you have all of the phone numbers or addresses that you need, and any information or items that will be part of your errand-running or shopping stops.

Prepare as much as possible the things that you intend to include in a sack lunch. Sort things out for easy assembly the following morning.

As you undress, put your clothes immediately into the proper laundry hampers, and insist that your children do the same.

If you have any personal care routines, do them before you go to bed. You'll do a better job than if you try to do them as part of the morning rush.

If you need to, set two alarms—one of which is across the room.

You'll probably sleep easier knowing that you've already got a running start on the next day, and you'll be far less likely to forget something in the hurry of the next morning.

INFORMATION CONTROL

Nine quick and simple ideas
for managing the flow of communication
in your life and family

36 ✔ Mail Control

A few simple principles can help you dramatically in controlling the amount of paper you receive through the mail.

Eliminate the Junk If you are tired of having to deal with vast amounts of junk mail, you can write: Mail Preference Service, Direct Marketing Association, 6 East 43rd Street, New York, NY 10017. They will see that your name is no longer sold to large mailing list companies. This one step alone can reduce your junk mail by nearly half.

If you order from a catalog, and the order form has a box that says, "I prefer my name not be made available for special offers of similar merchandise," check the box.

Deal with Every Piece of Mail Only Once Immediately sort the mail as it comes in. If you can tell by the envelope that the contents are soliciting a donation or purchase, and you know you aren't interested, tear the envelope in half through your name and address and pitch it.

Put bills in a bill-paying pile to be opened and processed later.

Lay aside magazines, journals, and catalogs. Don't even open a magazine unless you plan to read or look through it thoroughly and then discard it. If you have no interest in a catalog, toss it, unopened.

Open first-class letters and business mail only when you have time to read through it fully. (You may want to stick it in your tote for reading during a spare minute of your day.)

Know When to Toss It   Throw away thank-you notes after you've read them. Don't keep birthday cards or greeting cards longer than a week. They're fun to look at, but unnecessary to store.

Discard packaging. If possible, recycle cardboard. You might want to devote a large trash bag to storing foam peanuts. Use that material, rather than newspaper, to cushion items you send.

Limit Your Subscriptions   Only subscribe to those publications you actually read. If you find an article in a magazine that you want to read, but don't have time to read it in its entirety, tear out the article and toss the rest of the magazine. If you can't seem to bear throwing out a magazine, remove your name and address from it and leave it in a laundromat or waiting room.

Don't save daily newspapers past midnight. Pitch them into a recycling bin.

As soon as you receive a catalog, toss its predecessor. As soon as you've looked through a catalog and decided against making any purchases, toss it. If you find an item you might like to purchase, tear it out, along with the order form, and put it in your to-buy file. Don't keep a catalog beyond the season of its issuance.

Develop Skimming Skills   If you are a slow reader, consider taking a speed-reading course. You can save yourself lots of hours in the course of your life, and learn more at the same time.

Learn to read headlines and subheads, first paragraphs, quotes and captions, as a fast way of getting an overview.

37 ✔ Keep a Daily Set of Files

As you process mail and information on a daily basis, put items into one of these five file folders, which you may want to keep handy in your office or kitchen in a hanging file system:

The To-Do File Invitations that need a response, recipes to try, correspondence to answer —these are the types of items to put in your to-do file. Include information about movies, concerts, seminars, or other events you may want to consider attending. Also include in this file the names and addresses of places you may want to write for information. Process this file at least once a week.

The To-Pay File Bills and subscription renewal forms go here. This is also the place to put your receipts from purchases made. Deal with this file at least once a week.

The To-Buy File Clippings from catalogs, newspapers, or magazines go here. Evaluate this file at least once every few weeks. If you find that you are no longer interested in an item or an event, toss the information about it.

The To-Read File Articles, brochures, and newsletters go here—but only if you really want to read them. Carry this file with you in your briefcase, tote, or carry-on luggage. After you read an article, toss it.

The To-File File Make sure you really need to keep the information you put into this file. Certain business records and research for future projects are readily justifiable. Most information should probably be tossed, not filed. The only reason to file an item is if you anticipate you'll need to refer to the information within the next six months. If you think your reference point is likely to be longer than that—and it isn't a document you may need for tax or long-range business purposes—toss it. The information probably won't be current enough for your purposes. Discipline yourself to empty this file at least once a week.

38 ✔ Label It

Develop the habit of labeling or identifying items clearly. You'll save yourself time and frustration.

- Label the contents of boxes you store in closets, basements, or garages.

- Identify the people, places, and dates associated with photographs. Write gently with a pen on the back of the photograph or along the side of a slide. You may think now that you'll always remember the names of the people in the photograph or the year it was taken, but you won't!

- Keep a running list of the items in your gift container.

- Label and date items you put into your freezer. It's difficult to tell the difference between beef stew and chili after the concoction has been frozen for a while.

- Label all keys.

- Write your name in books you want to keep, on the inside of the front cover, rather than on a page that might be torn out.

It only takes a few seconds to prepare and attach a label or a descriptive statement. Those few seconds can save you hours of search-and-remember time later.

39 ✔ Have One Central Message Board

Have a central place in your home where you can leave or receive messages. This family bulletin board should be located adjacent to the master family calendar. Both should be close to a phone. Make certain that pens and small pads of paper are readily accessible.

Get into the habit of putting the person's name in bold letters at the top of a message. If the message is for everybody in the family, write *everybody* or *you*.

Develop the habit of consulting the message board when you enter the house. As you leave home, develop a habit of jotting down where you have gone, what time you are leaving, when you expect to return, and how you can be reached.

Remove messages as soon as they have been received.

Keep a pen and pad of notepaper next to each phone in the house, and also by the side of your bed. That way, you'll be able to capture ideas and messages as they occur.

40 ✔ Medical Records

Medical information must be accessed quickly and thoroughly. In a time of crisis, there's no time to rummage through files. Here are six easy-to-implement suggestions that also have the potential for being life-saving ideas:

- *Post emergency first-aid information on the inside of a bathroom cabinet or cupboard.* Posters or charts are available that give quick summaries about what to do in case of burns, choking, allergic reactions, broken or sprained limbs, poisons, bleeding, fainting, muscle injuries, stings and bites. Be sure the information includes illustrated step-by-step procedures for the Heimlich technique and mouth-to-mouth resuscitation, as well as a diagram of artery pressure points.

- *Keep a simple first-aid manual clustered with your basic first-aid kit or supplies in that same cabinet.* Periodically check your first-aid kit to make certain that you have adequate supplies of tape, gauze, bandages,

and other items. Keep a similar first-aid kit
and manual in each of your family vehicles.

- *Keep all prescription medications clustered.*
  If you have young children in your home,
  make sure that they cannot gain access to
  prescription medications, or to any health-
  care product that might be harmful to
  them. Discard all out-of-date medications,
  empty bottles, or prescription medications
  that are no longer needed.

- *Carry with you at all times a list of medications that you or members of your family require.* Include the complete name of the
  medication, the dosage prescribed, and the
  prescribing physician.

- *Post the name and number of your primary-
  care physician on your central message board
  and leave it there permanently.* Teach your
  children how and when to use 911 to call
  for medical or emergency help. If 911 service is not available in your community, list
  the numbers to call for ambulance, fire
  fighting, or police assistance, and the name
  of your physician.

- *Develop a medical file folder for each member
  of your family, and keep it with your first-aid
  supplies and manual.* This folder should list
  the dates of immunizations, surgeries, and
  other medical procedures. It should include

names and phone numbers for all physicians regularly consulted by the person. Also list any medications that are taken on a regular ongoing basis. And, make sure that the file has the name and other pertinent information related to your health insurance coverage.

Having this information handy in an emergency can help a physician in diagnosing and treating a situation promptly and effectively.

41 ✔ Information Access

There's nothing quite as frustrating as not having the information you need, when and where you need it! Here are suggestions for bringing order to information.

- *Keep an extra copy of the phone book in your car.* It will probably slide easily under the front seat. If you aren't able to get an extra copy of the current book, carry the one that just expired. Tape a couple of quarters to the inside cover of the book. That way, you'll always have change for a call.

- *Keep a detailed and up-to-date map of your city and state in each family vehicle.* Teach your children how to read a map and give clear directions.

- *Make certain the operational manual to each vehicle remains within that vehicle.* Keep maintenance records up to date.

- *Have babysitter information clearly spelled out and made readily available.* Go over it with your sitter before you leave. Don't assume the sitter will find it or read it on her own. Be sure to leave clear instructions about what you expect the sitter to do. Tell where you have gone, when you expect to return, and how you can be reached. Show the sitter the name and address of your family physician. Show the sitter where you have put the medical files, emergency medical information, and first-aid kit. Give precise instructions about what you want the sitter to do if you cannot be reached.

• *Keep a record of the sizes worn by every member of your family at any given time.* Carry it with you among your lists. You'll save lots of time in exchanging clothing.

• *Cluster all warranties and operations manuals* for your currently owned appliances and equipment.

• *Carry your date book, address book, and lists with you at all times.*

42 ✔ Permanent Records

Here is information you should keep, and update periodically, as part of a permanent record of your life.

A Perpetual Calendar Invest in a perpetual calendar, a date book that gives dates but not days or years. Use this calendar to record births, anniversaries, graduations, baptisms, dates of death, and key dates in your business life.

A Gift Record Purchase a blank book in which you can record—by person—the gifts you have given and received. How many times have you purchased multiple items on a trip, only to forget to whom you gave them? A perpetual gift record can answer the question for you within seconds.

Holiday Card List You may find it useful to keep track of those with whom you have exchanged greeting cards through the years. You may want to indicate whether your relationship to the person is a business or personal one.

Entertainment Records   You may find it helpful to record menus and guest lists for specific parties or events.

A Master Address Book   You probably don't need or want to carry with you all of the names and addresses of people you have met, done business with, or are related to. One of the best ways to keep a master address file is to put the addresses on $3'' \times 5''$ cards. That way, the names are easily alphabetized, the file is readily expanded, and you'll also have room for making notes related to the person (food allergies or preferences, names of nearest relatives, or name of employer). Date the card, so that you have a record of how current the information is. Use pencil rather than ink so you can update addresses and phone numbers.

A Job Diary   You will probably benefit by having some record of when certain business transactions were conducted, projects were begun or completed, contracts were signed, items were shipped, and so forth. You can construct a job diary by taking a couple of minutes at the close of each work day and writing on your master calendar major transactions or work accomplished.

A Personal Journal Keeping a personal journal is an excellent way of recording the key events of your personal life and of gaining a perspective about yourself over time. Make regular entries. Note your feelings, the highlights of important conversations, your observations, and your opinions, as well as the facts about what you have done and where you have gone.

These permanent documents of your life will become your memory, and they will also give your heirs or survivors interesting insights into your life. Consider them to be historical documents. Be accurate and as complete as possible in your entries.

43 ✔ Purge Your Papers

Just as there are some documents and records worth keeping, there are others that should be discarded when their usefulness has expired.

Out-of-Date Information If information is no longer current, get rid of it. If you find warranties, operations manuals, or invoices related to items you no longer possess, discard them.

Old Files and Records Cluster vital business documents together. Chances are, the truly important business documents in your life (deeds, copies of your will, information about bank accounts, final wishes, policy numbers) can be kept in one expanding file. Consult your accountant or tax attorney for advice on how long you need to keep other business files and tax-related documents. Label your boxes or containers of business documents by year, and when you've passed the recommended time limit for keeping the documents, discard them!

Purge your file cabinets at least twice a year. If you haven't needed the information for the past six months, you are probably never going to need it.

Reevaluate Your Library Do you derive pleasure from having books around? Do you need books for research? Fine. But if books are taking up space you'd rather use for something else, start a give-away program. Contribute your unwanted books to a local school or charity that sponsors an annual book fair, or donate your books to a library, secondhand store, or senior citizens' center. The same goes for back issues of magazines.

Reevaluate your music, audiotape, and videotape libraries. Share information and music. Unless you're certain you want to keep an item for future reference or as a lasting reminder of your youth, pass it along to someone else who might benefit from it or find pleasure in it.

44 ✔ Simple Lend-and-Return Strategies

If you have items you don't mind loaning to others but you want returned, it will be up to you to make certain that you set up the best possible system for ensuring that the loaned items find their way home.

Identify Your Ownership of Books, Videos, Games, Tapes, and CDs Find a style of bookplate you like and invest in a large quantity of them. Affix them to the inside front cover of books, on videotapes you own (on the tape itself, not the box), on the back of audiotapes and game boards, on the inside front or back of CD holders. The first step in getting items returned is to let a person know clearly, at a glance, that the item is yours.

Keep a Check-Out Record You might want to keep a blank book in an accessible place so you can record the loan of a particular item. You don't need to call attention to the book or make a formal ceremony out of lending an item. Simply jot a line to yourself after loaning an item you want to see again. If the item is not returned in a timely fashion, you'll remember whom you need to call.

State Your Desire to Have the Item Returned   When you loan an item, state clearly, "I'd appreciate your returning this when you are finished with it. That way I can loan it to another friend in the future."

Potluck ID   When taking a dish to a group picnic, company party, or potluck dinner, be sure to label your container. Put your name on a bit of masking tape and attach it to the bottom of the dish so you can identify it later. Avoid taking your best china, silver, or sterling flatware.

Sharing with Roommates   Have a clear-cut agreement with any roommate about what is yours and what isn't, as well as what you are making available for communal use and what is for your own private use. Avoid purchasing items together. If you do purchase a lasting item that is for mutual use and enjoyment, such as a piece of furniture, appliance, or decorative item, keep a record of your purchase and date it.

LIFE SIMPLIFIERS

Eight strategies for
simplifying your everyday life

45 ✔ Limit the Traffic

Your home doesn't need to be Grand Central Station. Let others in your circle of friends, and your children's friends, share the responsibility for hosting, entertaining, and child-watching.

- *Limit the meetings.* Put a limit on the number of nights a month that you have meetings, groups, or parties in your home.

- *Limit the number of dinner guests.* Consider having only one night a week or one meal a week when you have a guest for dinner. Rotate the choice of guest among household members.

- *Limit the number of friends who come over.* More than two friends per child and you tend to end up with a party or a war. Take turns having friends over.

- *Limit heavy traffic to certain rooms in the house.* Keep children confined to a child's bedroom or playroom. Keep food and beverage consumption confined to the kitchen or outdoors.

- *Limit the number of sleep-over nights your children host* to an occasional guest or a once-a-year party. You don't need to host friends every weekend.

- *Limit access to your yard,* especially your swimming pool, outdoor gym equipment, or any athletic courts. You may be held legally and financially responsible for any accidents that occur in your yard or home. Make sure your insurance coverage is adequate. Insist that guests use your yard and pool only when you are present or on invitation.

Limit; Do Not Eliminate By limiting the traffic in your home, you are not necessarily eliminating people from your life or diminishing relationships. If your friends, or your children's friends, only like you because of your ability to entertain, they aren't true friends.

Limiting the level of traffic through your home cuts down on expense, frees up more of your time, lessens the wear and tear on your furniture and yard, and adds a greater feeling of peace and tranquility to your home. It's a compliment, of course, to have everyone want to meet at your house. Remain a gracious hostess—less frequently.

Limit Your Own Goings and Comings

Even as you cut back on the number of people who come into and through your home, attempt to limit the number of trips you need to make to and from your house. Run errands and make shopping stops en route to and from work or meetings. Share carpooling responsibilities with others. Use home-delivery services. You'll streamline the use of your time, spend less money in vehicle use, and probably feel a greater sense of order in your life.

46 ✔ Don't Add—Subtract!

If you haven't already added certain elements to your life, don't add them now.

Borrow a Pet If you don't have a pet, don't acquire one. Pets take a great deal of time, energy, and more money in food, veterinarian, and boarding expenses than most people ever stop to calculate.

If you have a pet, keep it outdoors, if at all possible. If you must have it indoors, place limits on where the animal can go in the house. It's twice as difficult to keep a room neat and orderly if a pet is allowed to use it.

You can always borrow a pet. Visit friends who have one, go for horse rides at a local stable, spend an afternoon at a petting zoo, walk the neighbor's dog, or even pet-sit for a neighbor who is away for a vacation.

Rent, Rather than Buy Rather than buy expensive sporting equipment that you might use only once or twice a year, rent it. The same goes for cabins, beach houses, or desert condominiums and camping gear.

Limit Your Collections If you haven't started collecting something, don't begin. If you must collect, choose something that you can use, like teapots or silver coffee spoons.

If you haven't already acquired sets of formal china, crystal, and silver tea sets or flatware, consider whether you truly want or need such items. Few people use their formal entertaining services more than once or twice a year.

47 ✔ Streamlining the Cleanup

Washing and cleaning up can seem like endless activities. The key principle to remember is that everyone does their share.

- *Everyone clears their own place at the table and rinses off the dishes.* Teach your children how to load and run the dishwasher. If you don't have a dishwasher, consider getting one. Until you get one, include your children in the wash-and-dry process.

- *Everyone puts their clothes into laundry hampers at the end of the day.* You can facilitate the laundry process by using multiple laundry hampers: one for whites, one for delicates, one for colored clothes. Stackable bins can make the sorting easy. Even young children can sort. And, if everyone pitches in—and pitches their clothes into the right bins—the laundry gets done much faster.

    Everyone should be able to do a load of laundry. Post very simple instructions for washing clothes in a visible place near your washing machine and dryer. Teach your children how to load the machine and run it, how to measure detergents and use fabric softeners. Teach your children how to sort out garments that do not go in the dryer, and how to hang garments on a clothesline. Let everybody, even your three-year-old, help fold towels and sheets.

- *Everyone makes their own bed, empties their own wastepaper basket, hangs up their own clothes, folds their own towels on the rack in the bathroom, and picks up their own room.* Children older than six can help in the cleaning process, learning to vacuum, dust, mop, and clean windows. Children older than eight should be taught to use an iron.

- *Everyone has "family help" chores.* It may be as simple as bringing in the paper and mail, taking out the trash, setting the table, raking leaves, sweeping off the porch.

Make the Most of Machines   Let machines work for you. Don't have what you don't need, but *DO* have what helps.

If you are in the market for a stove, get one with a self-cleaning oven. If you are in the market for a new refrigerator, get one that you don't need to defrost. If you need a lawn mower, consider one of the new models that mulches, and is self-propelling. Consider getting a dishwasher and a trash compactor.

Good Cleanup Gear and Clothing Invest in a good mop, a good ceiling brush, and good brooms. Have the brushes, pails, and scrubbers you need. Wear gloves when gardening or cleaning. Wear goggles or dust masks when you need to. When working in the yard, wear sturdy shoes and long pants. You may want to have a set of work clothes set aside for especially messy jobs.

48 ✔ Simplify Your Personal Care

Here are ways you can simplify your own personal care routines and possessions to save time, money, and inconvenience:

- *Nails.* Keep your nails short. Wear clear nail polish or buff your nails.

- *Hair.* Invest in a good haircut, and a perm if you need extra body. Choose a hairstyle that's simple to do and requires minimal fuss on your part. Cut down on the use of aerosol sprays. Your lungs, and the environment, will both benefit.

- *Carry-along supplies.* Carry duplicate containers of the beauty supplies you need in your carry-on bag, purse, or tote.

- *Don't self-prescribe.* If you develop skin problems, see a dermatologist. If you have questions about makeup, consult a makeup stylist at a department store or salon. If you have hair problems, talk to your hair stylist about them.

- *Use what works for you.* When you find a product that works for you, whether shampoo, deodorant, mascara, or razor blade, stick with it.

- *Gentle does it.* If you have sensitive skin, avoid deodorant soaps and highly perfumed products. Try hypoallergenic cosmetics.

- *Simple works.* Plain Ivory Soap and water work for most people as a way to cleanse and moisturize. Vaseline is still a highly rated skin protector. A mixture of baking soda and salt still makes an excellent toothpaste.

- *Good scents.* Find a classic fragrance that you love, and that loves you, and stay with it. Use unscented deodorants, hair sprays, and soaps. Don't confuse the aroma around you.

- *Mix and match.* Develop a wardrobe that has lots of mix-and-match separates: blazers, skirts, pants, blouses. Choose simply cut designs, solid colors, and classic weaves. You'll save yourself lots of money, and also find you have more versatility in looks for your dollar spent, less luggage to haul around on trips, a greater ability to go from dawn to midnight with just a change of accessories, and a better sense of style.

- *Lingerie.* Have enough underwear, nightwear, and hosiery to make it through a week. Always use the gentle cycle and low heat for items that have elastic or lace.

- *Shoes.* Buy only those that fit well and are comfortable the first time you put them on. Don't buy shoes with the intent of breaking them in; they usually break you first. Keep your shoes in good repair, replacing heels as you need to. Keep your shoes polished. Choose simple classic styles and low heels. They not only wear well, but they are better for your feet and back.

- *Accessories.* Become a master at accessories. They can update a wardrobe for a fraction of the cost of a new garment. Keep your jewelry simple and minimal; it will be more versatile that way.

- *Purses and wallets.* Choose ones of good quality leather, a size and style you are comfortable with, and stick with neutral colors.

49 ✔ Travel Light

Simplify your travel routines and you'll probably enjoy travel more, even boring business trips.

Carry It On   Carry on everything, if you can; you'll save lots of airport time. Travel light; don't take one ounce with you that you don't absolutely need. Keep your carry-on pieces to a minimum. The more pieces you juggle, the greater the likelihood that you'll leave something behind.

If you do check your luggage, make sure you have a change of clothes with you in your carry-on bag, as well as necessary personal-care products.

Travel Sizes   Use travel sizes of beauty products, or invest in small travel containers and fill them with your choice of products.

Coordinated Looks   Having a mix-and-match wardrobe will be a blessing if you are going to be away more than a day or two. Switch your blouse and scarf, jewelry and belt, and nobody will notice that you wore the same pants or skirt the day before.

Wrinkle-free Choose garments that resist wrinkles. Most hotels have irons and ironing boards that you can request from housekeeping, or ask the hotel valet to press a garment for you. It costs a little but saves you time and the effort of lugging around an iron.

Worry-free Leave cash and valuables at home.

Prepacking If you take more than one trip per month, keep a complete set of personal-care products in your suitcase at all times, along with a travel alarm clock. Keep a master list of "things to remember to take" tucked in your suitcase. It will save you hours of packing time, and you'll forget fewer necessities.

The night before, pack virtually all that you are going to take with you. If you are leaving on a family vacation by car, load up the car the night before. It you're traveling by plane, have your suitcases loaded and waiting by the front door before you go to bed, along with your tickets.

As You Go Take along a few plastic bags for storing garments that need laundering. Use shoe protectors. Have any major purchases shipped home.

50 ✔ Entertain with Ease

Think "simple and elegant" when it comes to entertaining.

Food Serve foods that are easy to prepare, easy to serve, easy to eat, and easy to clean off the carpet. Don't overload the menu; a few well-prepared items will suffice. Choose items you can prepare in advance. Get out of the kitchen and enjoy your own party!

Let others help. Barbecues are a great idea. Let some of the guests do the outside cooking while others do the inside preparation.

Encourage potlucks, with each person bringing a dish or beverage.

Decorations Use your own linens and objects you already own. Cut a few branches of greenery from your yard if you feel the need for a centerpiece of some kind.

Consider investing in clear glass dishes. Used with colorful placemats and napkins, they give you versatility in entertaining. Put a paper doily on a clear dish and you have a party platter for cookies or finger sandwiches. Slide a pewter or brass plate liner under a clear plate and you have instant elegance. Plus, they go through the dishwasher without any problem.

A Quick-Fix Party Shelf
Keep a few items on hand in a cupboard for drop-in, quick-fix entertaining. A few cans or jars (salmon, tuna, smoked oysters, nuts), a few unopened boxes (specialty crackers, pasta), several bags of popcorn, a few pouches of dried fruit, an extra jar of peanut butter and jelly, and chances are, you have all that you need to throw together a light meal or quick snack for guests of any age.

Anticipate Spills and Spots
Use tablecloths. Have sufficient coasters available. Hand a person a napkin as you offer a beverage or food.

Back-to-Back Parties
Cluster your entertaining. Make double the amount you need, and entertain different groups of guests two days in a row.

Go Out
If you really don't enjoy entertaining at home, go out instead!

51 ✔ Always with You

In addition to the money, licenses, credit cards, keys, and personal-care products most people carry with them as routine, here are a few items that you are wise to carry with you in your purse, briefcase, or tote:

- A pocket-sized calculator.

- Change for a pay phone.

- A few postage stamps.

- A small notepad of blank paper and a couple of pens.

- A small repair kit that includes several safety pins of different sizes, a needle and a few lengths of thread in basic colors, and several bandages of different sizes.

- A clean handkerchief.

- A day's supply of the medications you need, in case you don't get back home in time.

- Your planning diary or master calendar, address book, lists, and claim checks.

- A small pocket knife.

If you are traveling through life with young children, you'll obviously need to have a few other items with you at all times. One of the most valuable is a dry set of clothes carried in the trunk of your car, including underwear, socks, and shoes.

52 ✔ Build Strong and Joyous Friendships

Choose to build strong and joyous friendships. In order to do that, you will need to limit your associations. In so doing, you'll also be limiting your obligations and responsibilities.

You simply cannot be a close friend to everybody. Friendships take time to build and sustain. In fact, you probably can't develop, successfully, more than a dozen close friendships. Having four or five close friends is more likely. Having even one close friend is a blessing!

Don't feel a need to socialize with people because you work with them, or worship with them. Choose to build friendships with people you truly enjoy being with. Cultivate these relationships. Nurture them. Find innovative and creative ways of helping them, blessing them, encouraging them. Give to them. Be there for your friends in times of crisis, in ways that are meaningful to them. And learn to receive from your friends.

What does all of this have to do with an ordered life? It has to do with balance, fulfillment, and joy.

Build friendships that are mutually supportive,

marked by open communication, trust, and laughter.

There's nothing that gives more joy to life than a long-lasting, mutually rewarding, enriching friendship. Order your life to include friends as a top priority!